AF251753

HOME AGAIN

A CELEBRATION OF
WATSON BROWN'S RETURN
TO VANDERBILT

By
Wallene T. Dockery

SPORTS MARKETING, INC.

PUBLISHERS DATA

Design and selection ©1986 Sports Marketing, Inc.
Compilation of quotations and illustrations ©S.M.I.

All rights reserved. This book may not be reproduced, in whole or in part, in any form, without permission. Inquiries should be addressed to Sports Marketing, Inc., 2734 Hunters Forest, Germantown, Tn. 38138.

Due to the nature of the subject matter, Sports Marketing, Inc., makes no claim as to the originality of any material contained herein.

First Edition.

Library of Congress Catalog number 86-061417.

Published by ©S.M.I. in the United States of America, 1986.

ISBN 0-936169-02-8.

ACKNOWLEDGEMENT

Metropolitan Federal is happy to support Vanderbilt and Watson Brown through this special book, **HOME AGAIN**. This modern day love story of a coach and his alma mater will prove a valuable addition to your library.

On behalf of the board of directors, officers and employees of Metropolitan Federal, we are proud to have had a part in presenting **HOME AGAIN** to our community.

Edwin W. Moats Jr.
President
Metropolitan Federal

Vanderbilt Stadium

TABLE OF CONTENTS

Watson Brown at press conference announcing
his return to Vanderbilt.

INTRODUCTION

"You can't set your watch by your dreams.
They operate on schedules of their own."
— "Perfect Strangers"

In 1967 a lanky, tousled-haired high school All-American signed a football grant-in-aid with Vanderbilt University, which turned out to be more than the standard four-year commitment. With the flourish of his pen, Watson Brown also gave away his heart and sealed his athletic destiny in a way no one could possibly foresee. He dreamed of bringing fame to the Commodores with his highly recruited skills as a quarterback. Fate had another path in mind.

Certainly, the union began in a story-book fashion. Watson directed Vandy's 1968 freshman team to an undefeated 5-0 season. As a sophomore he captured two national back of the week honors and the Southeastern conference pass completion percentage title.

However, Watson's dream came untracked his junior year. An ugly shoulder injury, following a knee injury, produced a permanently lame arm. For all intents and purposes, Watson's athletic career was over.

The period that followed was dark. Watson struggled to make a come-back. He failed again and again. Unbeknownst to him, fate had thrown a detour sign in his path. Like a sword molded by fire, Watson's future was being readied for greater things... as Vanderbilt's future football leader.

First, Watson was befriended by the late Jess Neely, a former Vandy player who was the beloved Commodore athletic director and golf coach. Coach Neely saw the potential as well as the despair in the permanently side-lined athlete. He gave Watson his collection of playbooks. He offered encouragement, too.

Watson Brown greets well-wishers after press
conference.

INTRODUCTION

The next fall, in order to finish his degree, Watson signed on as a graduate assistant coach under Vandy's youthful Steve Sloan. Football became fun again, and Watson finally realized what Coach Neely had recognized all along — that he was meant to coach.

He sailed away to make his mark in the world — to East Carolina, Jacksonville (Ala.) State, and Texas Tech as an assistant, then to Austin Peay State as the nation's youngest head coach at 28 years old.

Vanderbilt still held his heart, and once again the lure proved too strong. Watson returned home as offensive coordinator in 1981 to direct two of the most exciting football seasons in modern Vandy history.

The timing still wasn't right. Watson left home again, spending one season as Cincinnati's head man and two as the highly paid athletic director/head coach at Rice. And suddenly, his journey came to an end. He had reached his dream.

On December 5, 1985 — 18 years after he had signed over his destiny to the Commodores — Watson Brown came home. For the first time in 38 years Vanderbilt football would be directed by one of its own. Vanderbilt fans rejoiced. So did Brown.

"We love it here, and we'll never leave again," he said, joyfully. "This is home. This is what I've always wanted."

This is what Coach Neely must have wanted, too. Somewhere, somehow... he has to be smiling.

— Wallene Dockery

FAMILY

The Brown family, November 1967.

Seems like Watson's been calling plays all his life. When he was a senior, Cookeville played Clarksville in the Civitan Bowl. During the third quarter Coach Bucky Pitts called a time-out, and Watson walked over to the sideline.

"What are you gonna run?" Coach Pitts asked.

"I don't know."

"Well, get back out there, and make up your mind," Coach Pitts said.

Watson did. Cookeville won, notching an undefeated season and a number two ranking in the state.

— Melvin Brown, father

When Watson was ten years old, he, his brother Mack, and Kevin Tucker organized a neighborhood football game to raise money for the Red Cross. They sold tickets, had programs printed, and even sold lemonade. Eight boys played on each team, because that's all Watson could round up. The next day the boys dressed up in their uniforms and took the $20 to the Red Cross office. The local paper took their pictures... and that was Watson's first exposure to the press!

— Katherine Brown, mother

Vanderbilt publicity picture: Mack, left, and
Watson.

Watson and I were always best friends. We played together from the time we could walk, and we developed an unusual awareness of each other during game situations.

When Watson was a senior quarterback, I was the junior receiver. Bucky Pitts, our coach, designed a run-and-shoot offense for us that consisted of, "Mack, you get open. Watson, you throw to him." During games in the huddle Watson would say, "Mack, go down 10 yards and hook." When I did, the ball would always be there. I caught 66 passes that year, and we were undefeated.

I went on every recruiting trip with Watson. I sat in Coach Bryant's office and heard him tell Watson that he would be Alabama's next All-American. The next year I followed Watson to Vanderbilt, because I felt we could do the same thing we had done in high school. It didn't work. Watson hurt his knee and shoulder. No longer could I just run downfield and wait for Watson's passes. Now I had to learn three different reads for a pass route plus all the components of the offense, and I had trouble adjusting. Finally, after my sophomore spring practice, I transferred to Florida State. It was a hard time for us. For the first time in our lives, things didn't work out like we planned.

— Mack Brown, brother
Tulane Head Coach

The Brown brothers: Mel, a sophomore at Cookeville High, is flanked by Watson, right, a sophomore at Vanderbilt and Mack, a freshman at Vanderbilt.

I always wanted my boys to grow up with a sense of compassion and sensitivity. When Watson and his two younger brothers were little, I gave them plaques for their rooms which read:

"What you are is God's gift to you.
What you become is your gift to God."

Years later during Watson's first speech as a head coach, I cried when he told the audience how much that message had influenced his life. I realized that he had become all I had wished for him... and more.

— Katherine Brown, mother

Watson Brown, 12, at Mickey Owens baseball
camp, Joplin, Mo.

When Watson was little I once made the mistake of reading him a story about a deer who had caught its foot in a steel trap. He cried big, sympathetic tears. From then on I was careful to choose better reading material.

Watson attended a Mickey Owen baseball camp when he was nine. Afterwards, on family houseboat outings, Watson would take a pile of rocks on deck for batting practice rather than swim or fish.

He used to be a worrier, but he has outgrown that to some extent. Now his philosophy is, "Everyone has a chance to make it if he tries."

When Watson lived in the dorm at Vanderbilt, I used to take him stacks of prune cakes. Now his favorite "grandmother" food is beef stew and chocolate pie.

— Mary Ellen Watson, grandmother

Watson Brown's No. 14 jersey was retired at Cookeville High.

Watson only weighed 115 pounds as a (high school) freshman, but in the fourth game of the season, he was called in to relieve the senior quarterback. On the first play Watson handed off to teammate Billy Harris, who ran all the way for a touchdown. "At 115 pounds I intended for that to be the quickest handoff in football history," Watson always said.

By Watson's sophomore year, he was named starting quarterback. He only weighed 125 pounds. That was big enough for head coach Walter Jared. He was quoted in the paper as saying, "Watson has a lot of desire and surprising ability for his size, but he is so big in all the other ways that count, he will be able to carry the load."

— Katherine Brown, mother

Watson Brown takes a shot.

Family time was important to us when the boys were growing up. No matter how long their practices would last, I always delayed dinner so that we could eat together. Serving up three or four fried chickens for a 9 p.m. dinner was not unusual at our house.

— Katherine Brown, mother

When Watson was little, he spent hours on the floor playing with his football cards. He made up games and each card became a "player." Using all 10 of his fingers to run plays, he'd talk to his "players" all the while, praising them if they gained yardage or made good tackles.

— Mary Ellen Watson, grandmother

He was his own play-by-play announcer, too. He loved to talk about "long gainage." He would say, "The quarterback drops back... and it's a long gainage!"

— Katherine Brown, mother

FRIENDS

Watson Brown at Vanderbilt press day.

I'm one of Watson's biggest fans, and I have been since I taught him in the 4th grade. Because he was so dependable, he was always my class doorkeeper. One day my husband-to-be knocked on our door, and Watson answered. "Miss Sharpe," he said when he came back, "it's that man who thinks he's going to marry you."

Watson was a charmer even back then. The girls in our class had a Watson Brown Fan Club which met daily in the third stall of the rest room! But the thing that always impressed me the most about Watson was his patience. Even though he had outstanding athletic ability, he never minded including his less agile classmates on his team.

— Nancy Sharpe Woods
Former fourth grade teacher

Watson took a short stab at Vanderbilt baseball.

I coached Watson on two levels of baseball — as a Connie Mack All-Star and as a senior at Vanderbilt. He had been a great shortstop before his injuries. At Vandy I hadn't realized how badly his left shoulder had been damaged until he got hit between the eyes trying to snag a ball at shortstop. Because he wanted so badly to contribute, I moved him to outfield. Mid-way through the season, though, he broke his hand.

Watson's injuries ruined a great baseball career, but he still has that same great heart.

— Larry Schmittou
Texas Rangers Vice President

Watson Brown at Franklin Rodeo benefit, 1986.

Our friendship goes way back! My father and Watson's father played on the same high school Single Wing team together. When Watson was eight, he moved one house down from mine. From that point on we played together all the way through high school, where he was the quarterback and I was the end. All those years the Brown's backyard was our baseball field; the side yard, our basketball court; and the front yard, our football field. Their silver maples marked the goal lines on each end.

Watson is the most intense competitor I've ever known. He had to overcome adversity to even play. In grade school he developed polio in the upper muscle of his left arm. Because the muscle deteriorated, he had limited use of that arm. He never let it slow him down, though, and he became the local hero — an all-star in three sports. In fact, Bucky Pitts, our coach, took a bunch of us to play golf once when we were in high school. Watson had never played before... and he shot a 40 on nine holes.

— Kevin Tucker
Life-long friend

Watson Brown is laughing — not yelling.

One morning when Watson was a senior in high school I started down the hall to take a newly registered student to class. The floor had been freshly waxed, and I slipped, breaking my right wrist. Watson reached me first. He talked to me and stayed with me until I was taken care of, and then he checked on me every day until the cast came off.

— Bertie Buck
Cookeville High School Senior Counselor

COACHES
AND
PLAYERS

Vanderbilt head coach Bill Pace and his newest
signee, Watson Brown.

From Watson's first scrimmage as a freshman going against the varsity, I knew he was one of the finest option quarterbacks that I'd ever coach. He pitched the ball every which way — from behind his back, over his shoulder, with two hands — but it always wound up in the right place, and he always made the right decision.

Don Riley, our freshman coach, told me, "I can't coach him. He's too unorthodox." But I'd seen enough. "That's okay. You can coach the other quarterbacks," I said. "Turn this one over to me."

Our only problem turned out to be keeping him healthy. He developed a knee injury, a lame arm, then a fractured hand. He fought back hard, but just couldn't overcome it all. If it hadn't been for those injuries, no telling how good he could have been. Despite everything, he was a big factor in team meetings and morale. He was a fine leader.

— Bill Pace
Vanderbilt Head Coach 1967-72

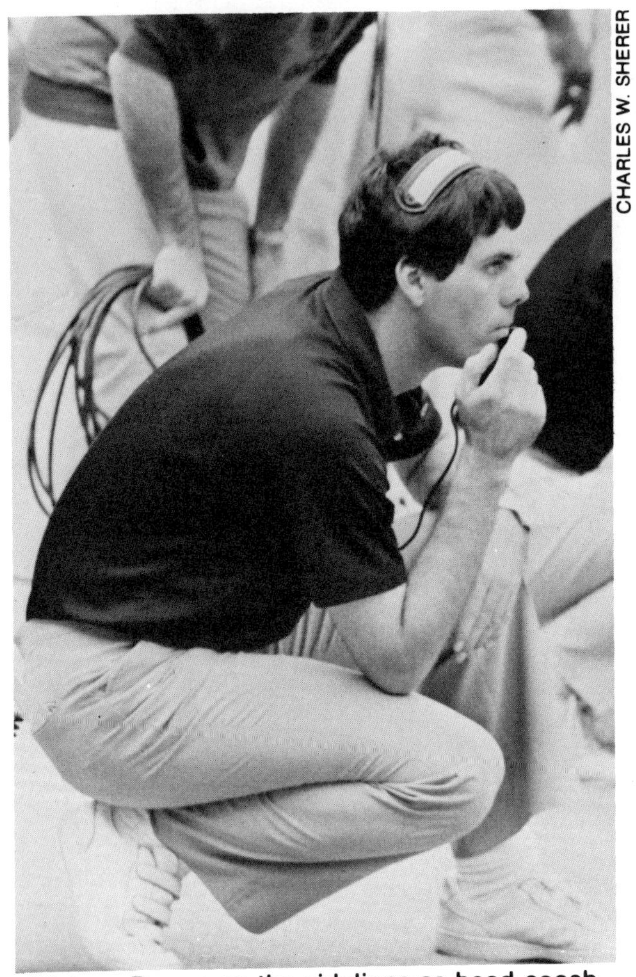

Watson Brown on the sidelines as head coach
at University of Cincinnati.

Watson is superstitious about pennies. He believes that if you find one heads-up, it'll bring you good luck. But he never picks up one tails-up. He thinks that's bad luck.

During our first season at Austin Peay in 1979 we won our first game, but we lost the next two or three in a row. Watson was feeling pretty low, until he found a penny. We won. He kept finding pennies... and we kept winning. We finished the season 7-4.

The next season we changed a few things offensively and defensively, and we lost the first couple of games. Watson was getting pretty uptight, so the assistant coaches decided to help out. We began hiding pennies where he could find them — in the coaches' dressing room, near his locker, in his office. Sure enough, we finished 7-4 again... and Watson never did figure out where all those pennies came from.

— Greg Mantooth
Vanderbilt Assistant Coach

Whit Taylor in a Vanderbilt publicity photo.

Coach Brown's tremendous game poise and concentration have always amazed me. When he was coordinator, we used an offense with lots of motion and shifting which took time to put into effect. That was never a problem. The second I got tackled or the play was dead, Coach Brown taught me to look at him on the sidelines for his next play signal. In two entire seasons I can remember only one delay of game penalty. That one was my fault. I was trying to check out of a play I had no business trying to change.

— Whit Taylor
Vanderbilt football 1978-82

Watson Brown and his coach, Bucky Pitts, after
winning a prep All-American football honor,
1967.

In the first ball game I ever coached at Cookeville, Watson was a junior quarterback trying to run my run-and-shoot offense. By halftime, he'd done so much scrambling, he'd already lost 150 or 160 yards. I told someone, "If I can just get to the fieldhouse at halftime, I believe I can help that boy."

Sure enough, we came back in the second half and tied the game. We had a good season that year and were undefeated the next.

Watson was real smart, and I let him run that ball club for me. He did it all.

— Bucky Pitts
Head Coach Guntersville (Ala.) High School

Brown and his troops before the 1986 Vanderbilt
spring game.

When Watson and I were graduate assistant coaches for Coach (Steve) Sloan's 1973 Vandy staff, we shared an office. At first Watson told me that he didn't know what he wanted to do with his life. By the end of the season, though, he knew. He wanted to coach.

I'll never forget the day he got up his courage and walked out to talk to Steve. He didn't have to go very far. Steve was looking for him, too.

"I've got Coach (Pat) Dye on the phone," Sloan said. "He's looking for a quarterback coach at East Carolina. You interested?"

That was all it took... and Watson was on his way to fame and fortune.

— Ken Hudgens
Vanderbilt Assistant Athletic Director

Norman Jordan in a Vanderbilt publicity photo.

During our first 1981 offensive players meeting, Coach Brown said, "I want everyone who believes we can have the number one offense in the conference to raise his hand."

Out of 45 players, only two hands went up. Coach Brown didn't flinch. "We can be first if we believe in ourselves, work hard, and do the little things," he told us, undaunted.

We thought he was crazy. We were a bunch of rag-tags who had been last in the conference for years... and here he was telling us we could have a great offensive team. Lo and behold, he was almost right. We ended the fall third in the SEC in total offense and first in passing. The next year when he asked us the same question, 45 hands shot up.

— Norman Jordan
Vanderbilt football 1978-82

Brown with Vanderbilt Athletic Director
Dr. Roy Kramer, center, and basketball coach
C.M. Newton.

Watson's one of those rare individuals whose charisma perfectly matches his university. To him, coaching football at Vanderbilt is not just a job. It's a way of life. His four years as a player and student gave him a deep affection and great pride in this school and became the signal call that finally brought him home.

Of all the people I've known, Watson's blood runs the truest black and gold.

— Roy Kramer
Vanderbilt Athletic Director

Brown on the sidelines at Rice University.

Watson was the best athlete I ever played with. The most competitive, too. Most ball carriers just try to keep from getting tackled. Watson played like he was determined to score every time... without getting touched.

In 1969 we had practiced all week in preparation for Tennessee's monster man defense where a defensive back lines up across from our tight end on the strong side.

Early in the game Watson had been knocked a little fuzzy while returning a punt. A few plays later (Coach Bill) Pace sent him in to quarterback. To Pace's surprise, instead of calling cadence, Watson called a time-out at the line of scrimmage and came running to the sideline.

"Coach," he said with a befuddled expression on his face, "they've got the monster man on the wrong side!"

Pace never missed a beat. "Well, then," he shot back, "why don't you tell Coach (Doug) Dickey to put him back where he's supposed to be."

— Doug Mathews
Vanderbilt football 1968-69

Watson Brown jokes with the press.

I first met Watson when we were both being recruited in high school by some of the same colleges,
and we became friends during the four years we played together at Vanderbilt. No doubt about it. Watson
has loved Vanderbilt from his playing days. And
through the years no matter where he went or how
excited he got about another job, I always knew that
this is where he wanted to be. His roots were here.
His heart is here... and for Watson Brown, this is home.

— Sandy Haury
Vanderbilt football 69-71

THE PRESS

Brown during spring drills, 1986.

I offer the prediction that Watson Brown will be Vanderbilt's head coach longer than any one since unforgetable Dan McGugin, who was on the job from 1904 through 1934. Brown is Vanderbilt's first alumnus since Red Sanders in 1948 and is more like Sanders than the seven other head coaches who followed. Raised in Nashville and a coach at Columbia (Tenn.) Military Academy, Red knew the territory. Watson knows it, too. The meadows and hills of middle Tennessee are a part of Brown's life, and Vanderbilt is the school where he has most wanted to be head coach. He's a perfect fit.

— Fred Russell
"Nashville Banner"

Vanderbilt vs. Alabama, 1985.

I once asked Gene Deflippo, a Vandy offensive staff member when Watson was coordinator, about the secret of Watson's success.

"He understands the opponent," he explained.

"When he watches the other team's film, he doesn't take notes, he doesn't speak. He just watches," Deflippo said. "After a while, he flips on the light. 'Now I understand what he's thinking,' he says. Just by watching, Watson can draw the defensive coordinator's coaching personality and is able to anticipate his game-time moves."

— Jimmy Davy
"The Tennessean"

Long-time coach, Eddie "Jelly" Watson, was
a big influence on his grandson's life.

Watson Brown had been in this world only a matter of hours before he had a football at his side.

When Brown was born in Cookeville General Hospital on April 19, 1950, his grandfather rushed over, beamed down at the tot that would carry his name, and carefully nestled a toy football beside the baby.

"He was less than a day old when I brought him that little football," recalls Brown's grandfather Eddie "Jelly" Watson, now 82.

"He was way too small to pick the ball up, of course. But that's how long he's been around one."

Chances are, football was already imbued in Brown's genes as intrinsically as his raven hair and dark eyes, but his grandfather was leaving nothing to chance. "Jelly" Watson, who coached football and various other sports for nigh 30 years, wanted to give his grandson more than his Christian name; he hoped to bequeath him his life-long devotion to the game.

That devotion has brought Watson Brown back to his Vanderbilt alma mater as head football coach, and with him an unprecedented aura of excitement around the Commodore program.

"All three of the boys — Watson and his little brothers, Mack and Mel — grew up on football fields, baseball diamonds and basketball courts," says the elder Watson. " I used to take them on the bus with me on road trips and they'd sit up in the front seat with me. They'd go with me to the dressing room and trail along behind me on the sidelines during the game. They were always right on my heels."

— Larry Woody
"The Tennessean"
Dec. 15, 1985

Vanderbilt's new uniforms for 1986.

When I think of Watson Brown, I'm reminded of the first time he made his mark on Vanderbilt's athletic fortunes. In 1969 Watson directed a Commodore ambush of mighty Alabama by throwing a touchdown pass for the 14-10 upset at Dudley Field.

After the game the press asked Coach "Bear" Bryant to comment about the loss. In a classic back-handed compliment to the former Cookeville All-American that "got away", he replied, "In three years (Coach) Bill Pace has brought Vanderbilt to the point it can beat Alabama. In 12 years I've brought Alabama to the point it can't beat Vanderbilt."

For his heroics, Watson was named "Sports Illustrated" National Back of the Week.

— John Bibb
"The Tennessean"

Long before Watson Brown was diagramming the X's and O's as a coach at Rice, Cincinnati, and Vanderbilt, he was daydreaming about football.

As a youth in Cookeville, Brown would sprawl out on the floor of his home with his collection of football cards. He'd lay the cards out in different formations and create imaginary gridiron battles.

"He'd sit for hours and play make-believe games with those cards," recalled Melvin Brown, Watson's father. "The rest of the family would be doing something in another room when, all of a sudden, we'd hear him yell 'Touchdown!'."

— Doug Segrest
"Nashville Banner"
Dec. 6, 1985

Brown makes a point during a press conference,
December 1985.

Why does Brown think he can be successful? Can he recruit more talented players than the ones going to Alabama, Georgia, Auburn, or Tennessee?

"Talent is important, but just talent alone won't always win," he said. "You have to find players who totally believe in what you are doing and have pride in your University."

Pride in Vanderbilt was a recurring theme in the initial press conference. No fewer than eight times did that noun come forth in the first handful of answers.

"When they run out on the field, if they look over at (the players from) Georgia or Alabama and wish they were wearing one of those jerseys, then you can't win. They have to have so much pride in the jersey they are wearing they will look at the player they are facing and think, 'I'm going to knock you on your fanny.' Once you get them there, you can win."

— Doug Williams
"GO GOLD — Inside Vanderbilt Sports"
January 1986

Spring game action 1986.

During the 1981 Vandy-UT Chattanooga game I personally witnessed the only time Watson Brown has ever been rendered completely speechless.

Up two touchdowns in the third quarter, Whit Taylor, Vandy's quarterback, dropped back on a quick out pattern from his own 20-yard line. The ball fluttered and hung in the air just long enough for a Chattanooga player to pick it off for a quick score.

The last person Whit wanted to see was his offensive coordinator. He headed for the other end of the bench, but like a bomb with a homing device, Watson zeroed in.

"Son," Watson bellowed in Whit's face, "Do you have money on this game?"

"Oh, no sir," Whit replied. "There's not a line on our game this week."

Watson sputtered and walked away, shaking his head. Whit recovered, his coach regained his voice, and the Commodores held on for a 28-14 win.

— Joe Biddle
"Nashville Banner"

Brown greets his Vanderbilt players after the first team meeting, December 12, 1985.

Early in 1982 during preparations for top-10 ranked Florida, Watson found a heads-up penny. Like most other superstitious coaches, he was convinced that it spelled good luck for his Commodores. On game day he showed up with that penny in his pocket. Whenever Watson thought Vandy needed something good to happen, he would rub it. Wouldn't you know — Vandy whipped Florida pretty good, and that coin found a permanent home for the rest of the season. In a Cinderella finish Vandy wound up tied for third in the SEC with a Hall of Fame Bowl bid. Watson thought it was due to the penny... but I know better.

— Charlie McAlexander
WSMV-TV

WATSON'S WORDS

TO WORK BY

Brown with Rice quarterback Kerry Overton.

IT'S ALL IN THE STATE OF MIND

If you think you are beaten, you are;
   If you think that you dare not, you don't;
If you'd like to win, but think that you can't
   It's almost a cinch you won't.

If you think you'll lose, you've lost;
   For out in the world you'll find
Success begins with a fellow's will;
   It's all in the state of mind.

Full many a race is lost
   Ere even a step is run;
And many a coward fails
   Ere his work is begun.

Think big, and your deeds will grow;
   Think small, and you'll fall behind;
Think that you can, and you will;
   It's all in the state of mind.

If you think you're outclassed, you are;
   You've got to think high to rise;
You've got to think sure of yourself before
   You can ever win the prize.

Life's battles don't always go
   To the stronger or faster man;
But sooner or later, the man that wins
   Is the fellow who thinks he can.

— Walter D. Wintle

The late Vanderbilt legend Jess Neely shakes
hands with team captain prior to coin toss.
Vanderbilt went on to beat Maryland 23-17 in
the first 1981 game in the new stadium.

I am no different from any other Vanderbilt alumnus. I sincerely cherish my Vanderbilt diploma. I know all the work that goes into hanging one of those documents on your wall.

I know our rules. I knew these rules when Coach Kramer called me. I know the university's attitude toward scholarship.

I believe football is but a part of the total campus experience. I know that it can be difficult to attend Vanderbilt and play football, but I also know it can be done. I have seen some outstanding players develop both in the classroom and on the field.

If I didn't believe we could win under the university rules, I wouldn't be coming home.

— Watson Brown
"The Tennessean"
Dec. 6, 1985

A coach who thinks he's got all the answers is about to get beat.

You're only as good as you think you are.

Woulda, coulda, shoulda — the "maybe" brothers — they'll get you into trouble every time.

Loyalty is the greatest trait of them all.

There is a big difference between winning... and winning with class.

A man rowing the boat has no time to rock it.

Winners don't always win, but a true winner does everything he can to win.

— Watson Brown

If you don't have a dream, how will you have a dream come true?

For every valley, there is a peak.

Winning is doing the best you can, regardless of the odds.

Bear Bryant with one recruit who got away —
Watson Brown — at Tuscaloosa in 1967.

Man's greatest moment is to be tested beyond what he thought might be his breaking point... and succeed.

— Paul "Bear" Bryant

Don't cut down a dead tree in the winter. Don't burn bridges in negative times.

Winning is not everything. It is the only thing.

— Vince Lombardi

God's delays are not God's denials.

— Robert Schuller

Faith: when you don't know what's going to happen, but you strongly believe anyway.

Stay calm, cool, and corrected.

— Robert Schuller

 Two All-Stars: Mack, left, and Watson.

But they that wait upon the Lord shall renew their strength. They shall mount up with wings like eagles; they shall run and not be weary; they shall walk and not faint.

— Isaiah 40:31

There is no gray area — you are either a winner or a loser. If you try to straddle the fence, you will fall off on the losing side every time.

— Watson Brown

A person who is afraid to lose is a person who has not prepared to win.

Doing your best is better than being the best.

> — Cathy Rigsby's mother

Hard work leads to confidence.

Our football team will always carry an air of positive nastiness.

> — Watson Brown

Watson Brown contemplates a question during
a Dec. 12, 1985 press conference.

It's not the critic who counts, nor the man who points out how the strong man stumbled, or where the doer of deeds could have done better. The credit belongs to the man who is actually in the arena; whose face is marred by dust and sweat and blood; who strives valiantly; who errs and comes short again and again; who knows the great enthusiasms, the great devotions, and spends himself in a worthy cause; who, at best, knows in the end the triumph of high achievement; and who, at the worst, if he fails, at least fails while daring greatly, so that his place shall never be with those cold and timid souls who know neither victory nor defeat.

— Theodore Roosevelt

Watson Brown talks with Michael MacIntyre,
son of George MacIntyre, the man Brown
replaced as head coach.

Lord,
give me the guidance
to know
when to hold on
and
when to let go
and the grace
to make the right decision
with dignity.

— Robert Schuller
Tough Times Never Last, But Tough People Do!

Character is class, respect, and loyalty. Character is having great pride in yourself, but at the same time, having humility for the role you must play within your environment.

— Watson Brown

Never let a problem become an excuse.

— Robert Schuller

Never look back, because somebody might be gaining on you.

— Satchel Page

The first step in whatever you are setting out to accomplish is the toughest step.

There is a big difference in confidence and arrogance.

Obviously, the play didn't work.

For anything nice, there is a price.

Great people are ordinary people with exhausting amounts of determination.

You don't sing with your mouth. You sing with your heart.

— Bing Crosby

Brown, right, on sidelines with head coach
George MacIntyre and quarterback Kurt Page.

Success comes quickly when nobody cares who gets the credit.

IF

If you can keep your head when all about you
    Are losing theirs and blaming it on you;
If you can trust yourself when men doubt you,
    And make allowance for their doubting, too;

If you can wait and not be tired of waiting,
    Or, being lied about, don't deal in lies;
Or, being hated, don't give way to hating;
    And yet don't look too good, nor talk too wise;

If you can dream, and not make dreams your master;
    If you can think, and not make thoughts your aim;
If you can meet with Triumph and Disaster,
    And treat those two imposters just the same;

If you can bear the truth you've spoken
    Twisted by knaves to make a trap for fools,
Or watch the things you gave your life to, broken,
    And stoop, and build them up with worn-out tools;

If you can make one heap of all your winnings
    And risk it on one turn of pitch-and-toss,
And lose, and start again at your beginnings
    And never breathe a word about your loss;

If you can force your heart and nerve and sinew
    To serve your turn long after they are gone,
And so hold on when there is nothing in you
    Except the Will which says to them: "Hold on!"

If you can walk with crowds and keep your virtue,
    Or walk with kings — nor lose the common touch —
If foes nor loving friends can hurt you,
    If all men count on you — but none too much;

If you can fill the unforgiving minute
    With sixty seconds' worth of distance run,
Yours is the Earth and everything that's in it,
    And — what is more — you'll be a Man, my son!

— Rudyard Kipling

For when the One Great Scorer comes
To mark against your name —
He writes, not that you won or lost,
But how you played the game.

— Grantland Rice
Vanderbilt 1901

I don't want our players to be intimidated by anything or anybody. That's one reason why I don't want them to use grades as a crutch for not winning football games. I want them to believe they can win in everything they do. That includes winning every time they step on the football field.

— Watson Brown
"GO GOLD — Inside Vanderbilt Sports"
January 1986

MILE
MARKERS

Watson with one of his biggest fans, his
daughter Gini.

1950   April 19, born in Cookeville, Tenn., to Melvin and Katherine Brown.

1965-66   As a sophomore, became starting quarterback at Cookeville High School under head coach Walter Jared. All-district in basketball and baseball.

1966-67   As a junior quarterback under head coach Bucky Pitts, named Mid-State All-Star of the Week and ranked in top 20 in scoring in Middle Tennessee. Junior class vice president, Boys State Representative, U.S. Jaycees Scholastic Achievement Award winner, and all-conference basketball.

1967-68   Team co-captain. Directed an undefeated season, a Civitan Bowl victory over Clarksville, and a No. 2 ranking in the state. Selected All-State, All-American, Mid-State Player of the Year, and Special Leadership Award winner. Football jersey, No. 14, officially retired by Cookeville High School. Offered pro baseball contract with Boston Red Sox. Named Cookeville High School's "Mr. Cavalier".

1968   Led Vanderbilt freshmen team to 5-0 record with 379 yards passing and 484 yards rushing.

1969   As a sophomore quarterback, named "Sports Illustrated" National Back of the Week after 14-10 upset of Albama, SEC Back of the Week after a 42-6 win over Kentucky. Finished season as SEC pass completion leader with 62 percent (91 of 111). Selected Vandy's most valuable player.

1970   During second game of junior season, sustained knee injury in 52-0 win over The Citadel, and later, a severe shoulder injury.

1971   Redshirt year.

Brown on the sidelines with the late Rex
Dockery during a tense moment at Texas Tech.

1973	Graduate assistant coach under Steve Sloan. Received a B.S. degree in geology from Vanderbilt.
1974-75	East Carolina assistant offensive coordinator/quarterback coach under Pat Dye.
1975	Feb. 17, married Brenda Arnold.
1976-77	Jacksonville (Ala.) State offensive coordinator under Jim Fuller. Records of 7-4 and 11-3. Gulf South Conference Assistant Coach of the Year honors in 1977.
1977	July 26, daughter, Katherine Virginia (Gini) born.
1978	Texas Tech quarterback/receivers coach under Rex Dockery. Coached Ron Reeves to Southwest Conference Newcomer of Year award.
1979-80	Head coach at Austin Peay State and nation's youngest at 28. Two 7-4 seasons and twice runner-up Ohio Valley Conference Coach of Year. 1980 team led OVC in offense.
1981	As Vanderbilt's offensive coordinator under George MacIntyre, inaugurated new stadium with 23-17 upset victory over Maryland. Broke 30 school records. Finished season No. 1 in SEC passing and No. 8 in nation.
1982	Broke 27 school records. 8-4 season tied Vandy for 3rd in SEC, and a Hall of Fame Bowl bid against Air Force. No. 1 in SEC passing and No. 13 in nation.
1983	Head coach and athletic director of Rice University.
1984-85	Jan. 3, son Steven Arnold, born.
1985	Dec. 5, 35-year-old Brown returned home as the first Vanderbilt alumnus head coach in 38 years.

EPILOGUE

I expect to be here as long as folks will have me. I guess it's the going away that makes you appreciate the coming home.

— Watson Brown